T0148991

SANCTUARY

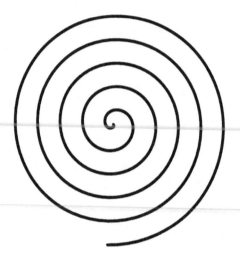

SANCTUARY

There Must Be Somewhere

Angela Graham

with

Phil Cope, Viviana Fiorentino,
Mahyar, Csilla Toldy, Glen Wilson

Seren is the book imprint of
Poetry Wales Press Ltd.
Suite 6, 4 Derwen Road, Bridgend, Wales, CF31 1LH

www.serenbooks.com
facebook.com/SerenBooks
twitter @SerenBooks

The right of Angela Graham to be identified as
the author of this work has been asserted in accordance
with the Copyright, Designs and Patents Act, 1988.

Editorial and her poems © Angela Graham, 2022
Individual poems © their authors, 2022

ISBN: 9781781726785
Ebook: 9781781726914

A CIP record for this title is available from the British Library.

All rights reserved. No part of this publication may be reproduced,
stored in a retrieval system, or transmitted at any time or by any means,
electronic, mechanical, photocopying, recording or otherwise without
the prior permission of the copyright holder.

The publisher acknowledges the financial assistance of the Books Council of Wales.

Printed in Bembo by Severnprint Ltd, Gloucester

Supported by The National Lottery through the Arts Council of Northern Ireland

Contents

It's urgent – Sanctuary. We live on an imperilled planet. The air we breathe is compromised by pollution and potential infection. Trust in authority and in one another has become harder to maintain. Is anything sacrosanct? What does 'holy' mean for us these days and what do we believe in? How can we be safe – and open? How are we to respond to war and upheaval? We need other people; we fear other people. How do we find our personal Sanctuary; or create it for others? And if we are fortunate enough to be in a safe place, who do we let in or keep out? What do we lose in return for our safety?

I was determined to explore these questions in poetry, but I wanted to create a set of poems which would embody that aspect of Sanctuary which is an opening up to give space to others. I realised I could ask other poets to join me. In addition, if I had to seek safety somewhere strange to me, I'd hope that local poets would welcome me and let me offer my poetic culture and share in theirs. As I live in both Wales and Northern Ireland, I sought a poet living in each place who has gone through this experience. I found Mahyar. He is an Iranian now living in Wales. Csilla Toldy is a Hungarian film maker and writer who fled communist Hungary and now lives in Northern Ireland.

I also looked for two poets engaging with other aspects of Sanctuary. Poet and novelist, Viviana Fiorentino is an economic migrant from Italy now living in Northern Ireland who is a social activist with migrants and prisoners of conscience. Welshman Phil Cope is a photographer and writer who is an expert on holy places in the British Isles.

But could we take a further step? Could each of these poets fashion their poem together with me? This collaborative approach proved to be a joyful, stimulating, delicate and very positive experience in each case. To be the first reader of a draft work is a privilege. To be permitted to engage at increasingly deeper levels challenges both parties but it proved to be akin to how I imagine the process of sculpting. There's a certain holding of nerve in order to deliver a critique or praise and a moment of tension as the result of that intervention makes itself clear. Something new emerges, is assessed, accepted or rejected and we go ahead in the pursuit of the true, the real, the poetically beautiful; and holding to the poet's core vision.

Collaboration with the Northern Irish poet, Glen Wilson took a different form. He acted as mentor to my poetry and contributes a fine poem of his own about migration.

My engagement with the backgrounds of the other poets and with their work has allowed me to learn about societies, cultures and experiences other than mine. This is enormously enriching, also in terms of craft.

I am inspired by the Welsh Government's ambition to make Wales the world's first Nation of Sanctuary. In Northern Ireland the Cities of Sanctuary Movement is developing.

At least five themes emerge strongly from the work in this book: Sanctuary in another person or persons; in the divine or the numinous; in the world, as itself a sanctuary for humanity; as the goal of major population shifts and in the response of receiving populations; as the hosting of the self within the body

I used to think of Sanctuary as primarily a place but this work has shown me that Sanctuary is also something that can be lived. We can be people of Sanctuary.   – *Angela Graham*

In my poem I wanted to explore the inner workings or imaginings of an illegal immigrant caught by border police, in this case at the border between Mexico and the USA.

Borders have come into a sharp focus in recent years with the rise of right wing nationalist leaders assuming power in some countries; Trump and his wall in USA; Russia's invasion of Ukraine bringing up issues of where people belong. The recent wars in Syria and Afghanistan and their inevitable displacement of populations has also been a crucial issue to respond to. I wanted to examine how the protagonist of my poem faced issues of belonging and culture as well as familial conflicts.

The treatment of refugees in the media made them appear to be aberrations, inherently different, whereas it seemed to me in my poem that dealing with familial issues would portray refugees as more than two dimensional. It would allow characters with depth to come to light and show there is a back story to everyone. I wanted my unnamed character to have agency despite the obstacles he faced, to not simply be another statistic.

There are many reasons why anyone leaves their country, negative reasons such as persecution, war and famine but also reasons such as new job opportunities, new relationships. The spur for anyone to move countries is not always straightforward and often multi-faceted.

As with all fiction I can only imagine so much before I need further research to gain an understanding of the situations that faced people like my protagonist. I found that it wasn't comfortable (and rightly so) to put myself in the position to leave the security and safety of what I knew to strike out into the unknown with no guarantee that what you are heading towards will be better. – *Glen Wilson*

These are days of growing uncertainty when our confidence in our political foundations, in the survival of our planet and even in the continued functioning of our own bodies are being challenged on a daily basis. At such times, we are all of us desperate for the secure, the consistent, the communal, the beautiful. And while I often now find my own personal sanctuary in the hills which surround my house, we can clearly also find it in words, carefully arranged on a blank page or, even better, read out loud. I often work with children and young people, encouraging the creation and performance of collective poems. *Sanctuary* feels a bit like that, the sum of these very different writers' words adding up to something that is much greater than us all.

– Phil Cope

I felt honoured to be asked to contribute to this project, but I was, as always, dreading to face my own history and reluctant to go back so far in time into it. I thought I was a cheat. I was a refugee during the Cold War over thirty years ago in Europe, not now and not in the UK. Yet, I am going through a period of my life when I have to be a sanctuary for many: my ageing parents, my daughter, my husband. When taking the issue onto the personal level I realised the wider consequences of my defecting and also the huge responsibility it might mean for any individual or country to provide sanctuary. The microcosm was reflecting the macrocosm. It is a beautiful role, to be the host, the healer, the mother, the friend, the priest or priestess or the inn-keeper if you are mature enough to take the burden onto your shoulders. More often than not it is a task given not chosen. The more gracefully we accept it the more wholesome it becomes for all involved. The poem sequence I ended up with took me back into my teens and carried me on into the present. It was a journey of enlightenment, for which I am grateful. *– Csilla Toldy*

I'm enjoying the project and theme itself so much. I feel so lucky to work on it as, by its nature, the Sanctuary is a very current concept. In a century where our planet is put at risk and we are too along with it, it is urgent and essential to think of what is sacred for us, what we want to protect. Anything we protect is something that protects us at the same time but also makes us a whole community. Reflecting with other artists on this concept is giving me the possibility to expand my point of view or change it, feeling connected, being part of the same community where we imagine a Sanctuary, a place, a body, a state of mind where we feel safe or we give others the possibility to be safe.

– Viviana Fiorentino

I don't call myself a poet or a writer, I'm just simply Mahyar, a wanderer who is seeking love since I can remember. A wanderer who is giving love since I can remember. Love, the true one, the unlimited one.

I'm not a poet or a writer but I imagine, I imagine so I can create. I imagine and I share my imagination as it is, I don't change it, I don't trim it, just as it is, so one may call it a poem and the other one may call it a piece of writing or some others may call it nothing but they are the creation of my imagination and my imagination is the only thing that I have and I share it as pure and as honest as it is, in the name of honesty.

Angela asked me to participate in the sanctuary project and it sparked my imagination and the outcome was 'You'. I shared it with Angela and we went on a imaginative journey to know more about 'You' and it was an honour to meet Angela and be part of the work that she started. I have learned a lot from Angela and I have found a great friend who I can share my imagination with. All thanks to 'You'. – Mahyar

Collaboration:
Sanctuary Poets Send Their First Drafts

I think of the artist that I know
who places mirrors underneath the sky,
on a shoreline, in lake shallows, onto ice,
to catch the shifts of light,
rain showers, the slow slug's crawl.

Onto these limpid discs
poems of happenstance inscribe themselves
and her shutter-click anthologises them.
Look: I have one on my wall
– clouds pool in a perfect O
among ragged pools of sea in a sandy heaven:
a double-worlding image.

I have been given five veiled mirrors,
each pregnant with an image,
each caul'd and burgeoning,
pulling me to peel away that skin, and I
– I am imaged within an image,
looking down to a world that is swimming up to meet me
and up through depths towards myself;
I am lured in, thrust out, dazzled and enlightened.

Here I am, in dialogue with icons,
with these world-doubling images.

The Russian Invasion of Ukraine: First Day

Spreaders of dread, heralds of worse to come
the helicopters – one… three… now six –
hover in a ring, their noses down, tails up
like dragonflies positioning to prey, heads together,
the red roofs of a village close below:
these we could take as easily as any other
lives.

The non-com's mobile footage on my screen
lurches, tilts – how can she tell where the next one's
coming from? Blinded by noise she – but –
there! – the camera-focus locks and renders me
a witness to their obeisance:
these we are taking, lord, as easily as any other
things.

From those red-roofed houses debris billows up,
slow as the smoke of incense. At this un-hideable pain
the 'copters, with a ponderous grace, dip and lift
and turn and leave their payload in my mind
where it replays each gesture in that violating ritual:
hybrid machines we are – unreachable– who once were
men.

But I always glimpse the mobile-wielder's hand;
despite the obliterating noise I hear her high, thin, wordless
cries and I cling to this: that her whole being voiced – not awe –
but horror as she held to a human scale: pity and pain,
the very – only – bridges raptors must cross to ever be men
again.

Leaving the Bombed City

The mirror vowed to hide his image in its depths
— this would be its last face.
Already a fragment, it was just enough for him
to prop on the shelf and comb his hair in,
turning his profile this way and that,
smoothing the sleek sides, lifting the luxuriant crown.
Handsome, the mirror told him. *Looking your best.*

The mirror saw him heft his rucksack, pat his pockets,
turn his back on the shattered balcony, the punched-in walls
and leave. Through each of his twenty years, to him
the mirror never lied. Now its heart cracked,
even as it folded his features carefully away.
All things must die but a mirror's death takes centuries
in multiplied versions of itself — smaller and smaller shards.

That look of his — forever just about to leave
(as a bridegroom for the altar, a singer for the stage),
his self-respect, his incredulity (deep-down)
that the world could ever genuinely wish him harm —
that look the mirror held, amazed to find itself at last
a mother: loving, mourning, honouring
the heart-breaking courage of the young.

Since the Evacuations from Kabul

Must sanctuary now imply its opposite:
the open sewer beside the airport gate;
the foreigners' pragmatic rush to quit
(the loophole shrunk by each departing state);
the frenzied sea of documents, held high
to prove the right to have a promise kept?
A worthless currency, they prove a lie
— expedient, well-meant, swiftly side-stepped.

Is there a scathing truth we have to face,
that outside every sanctuary there's a hell
where howling crowds who crave the sacred space
clamour to join the saved? Prison cell
and sanctuary — keys turn, locks click, bolts slide
but only one can open from inside.

A Heerd tha Sodjer on tha Radio

His wurds… an A wus thair!
Kabul, at a 'gate' in tha airdrome waa
 − a gap nae braider nor ma shoodèrs −
fornenst a thrang o despert fowk,
me atween thaim an 'oot'.

A wumman, wi hir babbie
ticht tae hir breesht,
püt hir left han tae ma face,
in that oul, oul leid that ses, aa tha worl roon,
Sodjer, be kine; tak peety on me…

Like that − somebodie mad a sprachle tae git ower tha waa,
tha hale crood riz, a wave
 − braithe, bodies, banes −
swep forrit. She wus doon!
A weltèr o feet an hans.

Somehoo A pu'd hir oot.
Ma billies hel tha line.
Safe in tha bield,
hir an tha chile
dee'd in ma airms.

Resilient, tha sodjer went. *We're trained to be… to be…*
Ach! Thair shud a bin yin wile lament, clocks stap't,
flegs loored! Thair's me in ma wee kitchen,
tha Ulstèr rain on tha wundae,
tha onlie 'mïnit's silence' his lang seech.

Scunnèrt tae ma sowl, A wus, wi shem.
Yin o a hirsel o herdless sheep,
forfoughen, thaveless.
Yit an wi aa, thon sodjer gien us his wurd o wutness.
Whut, then, shud we dae?

A went tae tha thrashel o ma kitchen dure.
Tha saft hans o tha rain. Ma face.
Thon oul, oul leid that ses,
Apen yer hairt
an let yer nighbers in.

Glossary

shoodèrs	shoulders
fornenst	opposite/faced with
leid	language
mad a sprachle	made an awkward lunge
beild	sanctuary/place of safety
seech	sigh
scnnnèrt	ashamed

Yin o a hirsel o herdless sheep, forgoughen, thaveless
One of a flock of sheep without a shepherd, exhausted, aimless

thrashel	threshold

Persian New Year

The table spread with symbols of spring –
I imagine that: سبزه، سمنو، سیب sabze, samanu, sib;
the hubbub of happy visits, the thresholds crowded,
your name in many mouths…
I can only imagine.

Let me give you gorse,
the ungraspable, the unlikely
solder-drops splattered on my hedges
by the sun torching its way out of winter.
Can you imagine?

You
Mahyar

Holy places and the holy books

No, they didn't satisfy me, they are not as they look

I've been looking for you, haven't I?

Gave me a familiar smile and asked me: why?

To live happily ever after

But I was there all the time, you answered me with laughter

The sound of laughter, the dark night and insomniac

I went deep inside myself with a dizzy flashback

To my Mummy Motherland, where I am banned

When I was enjoying the northern coast and the summer sand

Mum's kind cuddle, sweet dreams, far from reality

When dad's strong hands saved me from insanity

When I was writing a little love letter

When my eyes were getting wet and wetter

When I was drinking shot after shot

When I was reading Rubaiyat

When I was reading Khayyam's couplets

When the book got wet with my tears' droplets

When I was waiting restless

When I proposed and she said yes

When there was no hope and I was dazed

My child was healed, the doctors were amazed

When the world forgot me and life said goodbye fella

When I had nothing left except Maria's umbrella

When the army of thoughts was my mind's aggressor

Nobody understood me, there he came the humble professor

When I was close to the end and there were no ways

You hugged me and brought me back to life after three days

The more I reflect the more I remember

Yes you are right, you've been always there

Believe and enjoy your moments, just remember

I am always with you, I am always there

Consider

Why do you still call me 'refugee'?
Do you want me to be forever fleeing?
I have fled. Now I am here,
trying to keep both feet on the ground
and find my balance.

Sometimes I feel I have two hearts.
One, the first-created
— taut as a drum-skin in my chest —
trembles at far-off shifts of energy
in the fault-lines of the home I left.

The other has grown itself around the first
as lymph spreads on the surface of a wound;
as albumen, fragile, tremulous,
helps a new life mesh itself together
somehow.

I was a refugee. Now I am here
where I have to do so much explaining,
where I have to live so much on your terms
and I am growing this second heart
as bravely as I can.

Where I came from will always be
where I come from
and now I come from
— and so let me be —
here.

Border Crossing, Reynosa to Hidalgo
Glen Wilson

There is buzzing behind the bevel of the two-way mirror,
I imagine the voices of the hidden judges there,

they never reveal themselves, the faceless critics,
as border patrol officers ask questions in metronome;

Where did you come from?
Where were you going?

Looking clues to my genesis they have learned my language
for interrogation not exploration,

and they do not enjoy the rolled *rr* sounds
as they lose momentum through repetition in their mouths.

I rub my wrists, sore from the handcuffs, yellowed by corn,
a musician's hands my mother used to say of them,

everyone traces scars, knows their contours better
than the unblemished skin that has always been faithful.

In my family home there is a single picture of me,
making a sandcastle at the beach, bejewelled

with shells of long-left creatures,
defended by a shallow moat.

Did I disappoint my mother that I never built upon that promise?
Even worse do I disappoint that boy in the photograph?

His was a smile so easily widened with wonder.
Where was that wonder lost? The Atlantic?

Are we all doomed to disappoint our former selves
with dreams that track out with the tide?

Do the happiest of us acknowledge disappointments
and dream flatter dreams that tap the sap of experience?

It is like finding out we can dance without music or find God
reconciled in scripture and the resonance of a bumblebee.

I want to become the song I sing as it leaves my lips
up through Blue Oaks into places we don't even know exist.

The men tired of my silence leave me to echo in my defiance.

A Teenage Catholic Safety Expert, Protestant East Belfast

This house hasn't rooted in as yet
— its first full summer, 1971 —
but already Death has visited
and, outside, the garden's
a waste of undug mud
while your Daddy's car,
lonely in the driveway,
loyally grows moss
along its window frames.

This house was designed to let light in:
'picture' windows, wide triple bays
and a wall of glass where a stout
front door should be.
Such culpable naivety.
So turn your back on it,
close the three doors to the ground-floor rooms,
climb the stairs to the bath- and bedroom doors,
shut them and sit on the topmost step,
hugging the flimsy newel post,
its pristine gloss paint cool against your cheek,
its white on red.

Nothing can reach you here
but the shouts of children playing in the street,
so calibrate each call and cry
and hope that none goes past
the reckoning point
and if they stone the house
know this is the one safe spot.

Rehearse your exit strategy
— hopeless, yes, unless
some god would give you wings —
and never tell a soul
about your study of terrain,
of martyrdom, of dying well.

Glimpses

Sometimes – it's simple – you get glimpses, don't you?
Or
a sudden cloud between the sun and you
is the rehearsal of a future chill
or
there's your reflection in a shopfront window
and someone else's image joins the frame;
his face at your shoulder makes you turn
but he's surprised you think he thought
you were anything to do with him,
walks off, shaking his head, deeming you paranoid.
He's bluffing. You know
or
a dream, across the decades, re-presents itself,
twisting its facets, like a Rubik cube's,
to tease you towards its code.
In mine, a fire in my hearth
is a berserker
– white-hot core devouring the foundations,
arms thrust out to blaze right through my walls.
I shout, unheard, for expertise to tamp it...
wake at this crisis point.

In telling you these things, I've told myself
so I have to acknowledge now
that this is holy ground.
I have to
dare to gaze;
wrest from the apparition his true name;
claim the help I desperately need.
No burning bush for me
but these visions, visitations.

Chronic

The pain expels me from myself,
a fuck-thrust that makes me nothing
but spasm; blotted out.
Where do I go in these momentary rapes?

A Temple of the Holy Spirit, that's what your body is
they said at school, then slapped it well for minor faults
and praised those saints who treated theirs as nothing
but a beast to tote the precious soul.

And mine − where does my soul go
when the pain splits me apart?
I don't know where I am during these little deaths
but I return − so far − to the battered sanctuary

and find it a boxing ring
where the Holy Spirit is enshrined
on the ropes, pummelled,
holding out for me to make it back

and breathe; and breathe again;
number my bones, my spirit and my soul,
my memory, my agency and will −
all re-assembled 'til the next exile

but

there's no true exile from the body until death.
'Til then, without my body, I can't be
yet it hinders my being in the world,
calling attention to itself, obliging me
to learn the names of parts of it − of me −
I never had cause to think of
manubrium, conus, enthesis
insisting I draft a lexicon of pain.

What is your body telling you? they ask.
That it hurts, here, here and *here.*
But I am the one who's hurting.
Am I speaking to myself?

25

A poem inscribing itself in me,
intensely imagistic, denser than reason,
tells me I treat my body as
recalcitrant, suspect, lax — all things I hate;
as *bivouac*, as *bothy* or some kind of *lash-up*,
easily abandoned.

In truth, the body knows that I can never
do without it; that even at my death
the exile is provisional.
Though it disintegrate — in earth, in fire —
my body will encounter me again and claim me
for eternity.
So now, while time applies,
I must discover it
as *friend*, as *home.*

For Stephen, As He Leaves
for the Shrine of Santiago de Compostela

My field of stars
floats on the meniscus
of a watery sky
that I look up to.
Sun-glints on its surface
are my constellations;
my moon,
the shy side of a flower's parasol,
drifting. White. Fragile.

But yours –
you will recount
the stones, and dust,
the many beds,
the heat, and dryness
and the Gift,
pooling, drop-by-step
at the cowped jar's rim
to topple
gracefully
at your need.

cowped   toppled

Santiago de Compostela is the goal of the camino, the network of pilgrim-
age routes through France and Spain to the shrine of St James.

Another Lake, Another Land
Phil Cope

Poetry ... defies the space that separates ... reassembling what has been
scattered ... [equating] the reach of a feeling with the reach of the
universe.

John Berger
from *and our faces, my heart, brief as photos*, 1984

A brace of peregrines, monogamous
though solitary throughout the year,
rendezvous up here each April,
drawn by this cliff's magnetism,
egged on by legacy,
reliable in the knowledge of
a ledge, secure on Darren Fawr
to raise two chicks, then leave.

Swooping extravagant as sabres
a wing's breadth from
these bare rock walls
(cut first by mining's desperate
housing needs),
dead-stopping in
their hangman's caps,
the birds become the air,
preaching their gospel of the glide,
while benefits-scrounging off
the valley's welfare state of
starlings ripped open at the breast,
the occasional gull
crucified on claws,
an unfortunate pigeon,
small unlucky ducks.

These birds are fastest when
they're taking life,
fundamentalist in mid air,
hanging on to something
living, struggling, true,
at least for that one moment,

their quarry stunned by
a single savage hit
then slashing cleanly across
a soft and yielding neck.

Constantly redrawing
the atlas of the heavens,
these aerial cartographers understand
the rainfall's varied meanings,
the weather's moods and colours,
absorbing in their feathers
the merest rumours of
strong winds or storms,
offering the dream
of weightlessness
in the grip of the
certainty of death.

*

The Garw Valley's stones only ever fall
in one direction,
dead weights to a history which
mixes nature's skin and rivers' veins
within our nation's harshest and
most visible lessons:
the rocks, all synonyms for work
and suffering;
the wind, the finest antonym
for violation,
though clearer now of
mining's stink and dust;
our fossil waters running
clean and resurrected
towards the always-generous
arms of the sea.

Earth's urgent vocation
was interrupted here at coal,
before the pressures of
a few more millennia
might have presented us, instead,
a chest of diamonds to disinter.

Free falling like these stones,
this water,
these birds,
I'm remembering that lift
that Easter on our way to India,
hitch-hiking away from Christianity and
towards something else,
something out of reach,
sat on sacks of grain
in the back of a beat-up Turkish truck
crossing the bridge that crossed
the Bosphorus,
stared at by eyes that
wouldn't, we imagined, recognise
Big Ben or Shakespeare,
democracy or
even Jesus Christ, us two here as
voluntary asylum seekers after
a kind of simpler wisdom,
working backwards through
our dusty book of faiths.

We both confessed that night
that we had said something
like a prayer, fearing
in those moments for our lives,
our certainties collapsing,
challenged by this new,
this strange.

*

Billy'd watched the falcons fly,
so beautiful and cruel.
He admired their independence,
their sovereignty in
the kingdom of the empty air,
and dreamt, like me,
of soaring buoyant over
our school bullies (and his dad),
of swimming during playtimes high above

slate roofs, capped heads,
swooping in figures of eight and
perching, precarious, on gutterings,
though largely ignored by those below
despite our fantastic feats of
overcoming gravity and fear.

So Billy climbed one dawn to claim
two tiny oval suns, bursting
orange, red and brown and
promising something different,
something pure,
his fingers gripping hard on shifting rock,
feet searching out the confidence of
firm and level ground,
a ledge on something.

And while he pulled perpendicular,
against all reason,
up to his hoped-for little heavens,
some prophet in the valley below,
sliced off the top of
a breakfast egg and
a forest of new trees cut through
the fragile shell of that morning's sun,
spilling yellow over the new-born land.

Taking both eggs home,
proud to show his mam,
he found her angry at his crime against
the parenting birds (and all
our fragile human futures, too, perhaps)
and, being scolded,
climbed back up again
to the vacuum of the nest
to return his prizes.

But one missed hold,
one single loosened finger and
he's falling to the rocks' sharp rest below,
eggs and head and body smashed
on ancient quarried stone.

No fledgling birds this Spring,
no empty tomb, no Lazarus,
no boy to man.
The river only flows downhill.
Even if you are a bird
you only get one chance
to launch yourself
off this bone-picked shelf;
the smallest fraction more than
no chance
for a child.

Women washed the body in those days
but not the egg's stain off the stone:
this was the rite of rain and wind,
and as night fell, men,
used to digging harder rock,
dug yielding soil for
a single narrow grave.

★

I read somewhere that painters nearing
the completion of their canvases
sometimes insist upon
a viewing of their work within a mirror,
or even upside down,
believing that this might disclose
a purer form, a more real meaning.

The boy floated up
like a bird of prey or like a dream
beyond the sky's sheer walls,
living now only in the air's thin memories
as pages from a bright cloud library
were scattered by the breeze,
a biography unwritten, while,
far off, above Mynydd Llangeinor,
safe for the moment from
more human interference,
two birds rearranged
the atoms of the air.

Shadow-scarring the land in
their flight path eclipses of
dandelion and daisy,
of leaf and worm,
they watched the world, silent
through the rain's soft christening.

And in the wind- and
water-ruffled mirror of the lake
(above the pit that once dug our lives
and cut our throats),
the sky was still reflecting
charcoal grey and deepest blue,

and above the lake,
the real land, the real sky
sat unperturbed,
beyond our command,

and above the real sky,

another lake,
another land.

Triptych

The painter took my neighbour from his bed and nailed him to the wall, hammering his left hand, then his right, far apart on a wide crossbeam, pleating his feet, pinning them with a single blow – the body, hooked on its own bones, a sack of pain, sagging. The painter turned. His gaze raked our rows of beds. His finger pointed to the hanging man: *This is your God.*

At night I hear my neighbour, in his bed beside me, whimpering, or cursing. Sometimes he tears his suppurating flesh, screaming, "I hate you!" and the sisters have to bind his hands above his head. Then there are two men: one in the bed; one on the wall: *This is your God.*

I watch the morning light approach them. Neither sleeps. The one beside me stinks. The other twists against a blackness set to swallow him. His skin is greenish, every pore a mouth eating itself. He mirrors me: *This is your God.*

Am I, then, God? And is God me? I am that tortured one? The brothers retch when they tend me but they hold my eyes in theirs – as the painter did through those long days when he sat and watched us all; when he came and put his finger to my pulse and, for some reason, knelt beside me, suddenly.

Prompted by Grünewald's Isenheim altarpiece, a triptych painted between 1510-1515. The central panel depicts a crucified Christ contorted in agony, his body covered in appalling open sores. The painting was created for a hospital ward treating victims of a disfiguring skin disease. Their suffering and Christ's mirror each other. To Christ's left stands John the Baptist, his right forefinger pointing at the crucifixion. Behind the figures is an implacable blackness.

Three Stones

The message, when it comes, can't be mis-taken:
three stones, half-sunk in Cwm Garw sod:
a perfect triangle, two suns,
in white, in black − *Here is your God.*

My triptych: a nova, a black hole,
at the right hand and the left of the perfect Three
in lichen and in mottled reddish stone.
I am its shrine, my mind its sanctuary.

I used to try so hard to turn to stone
− I would at least out-last my torturers −
but, so I'd opt for flesh, God
became stone and met me where I was

− He always will − summoning me out
into the human self. O lichen
cosmos, O Trinity forever at my feet,
un-shutter me so that my gaze can listen.

Prompted by three photographs of lichen on stones in the Garw Valley by
Phil Cope, November 2020.

To the Mapper of Holy Wells and Springs

The question that running water asks
      – pools hold its gaze, reflecting, and rocks,
      under the frost's advice, consider
      its crystallizing, night after winter night –
you are right to believe it must be listened for;
right to condemn our mania for dogma.
Expert attendant, steady yourself.
Brim. Hear. Say, 'Yes'.

Prompted by *Offeren Y Llwyn*

In a lusty, rackety life delighting in the forest's maze,
its bolt-holes and thick complexities,
he stumbles, now and then, into a golden glade
where the plunging sun pinions him
and holds him fast so he can't fail to see
the words being lowered towards him on silver chains
like those that bubble in the wake of coins dropped in a pool
or the bright links that swing the censing thurible at Mass.

How the words settle, and mesh, and mantle him
till he smithies them into a poem,
a triad on *Where Sanctuary Is Found*:
>   between the thighs of woman
>   in the trees' cathedral
>   at the lifting of the host
and he gives thanks for the mercy of his God
who is human too.

Offeren Y Llwyn – The Woodland Mass – a poem by Dafydd ap
Gwilym. c. 1340-1370

Sanctum Trilogy
Csilla Toldy

Resistance

First it was a cave
the mother's body
   – then it must have been a den,
a blanket as tent hung over the table
or a hazel bush – remember that earthen home?
You the dad, me the mum.

Then it was to be found between the leaves of a book, I'm sure
a novel I wished was endless.
Later, the discovered peace of the church – forgiveness –
between party meetings,
dialectic materialism,
Lenin & Co., in the long shadow of the tsarevich
   – Alexei Nikolayevich Romanov –
a cherished boy with a blood disorder,
killed
by Bolsheviks.

This was a story you gave me. The brutality of detail
was your imagination.

ii

The heat of the sun still emanated from the asphalt,
we were sitting in a park, preferring the star-studded cave
of the night – a ferret ran through
embalming us in a moment of awe –
   – in my memory the church gates are open.
You knew even then that you
would die by suicide – it was written in the stars.
And all I wanted to do was to run –
away, back into that womb.
Instead, I took the road under my feet, saddened
the people I loved;
who believed that one had to die where one was born,
even if by suicide – obeying, if only the stars.

(Later I heard, your corpse was found
by a flatmate
– you bestowed on her a story, too.)

I sought sanctuary in the free west, forever misaligning my charts.
Seeing him – our friend – /who had Asperger's/ – (we just did not know
what to call it) –
       – a genius, I thought – buying army boots – as a metaphor for strength.
The weight of them grounding him in this new world
while he was a creature of flight –

                              even if his wings were not aligned.

iii

I wish to tell you, /if at all/, that he is, still alive.

Refuge

Sitting on the edge of our island,
the promised land for some
We, disciples, the fishermen
perform our burdensome task,
casting hook after hook.
    – We give you shelter, give you food
this is the free west, you are right,
but you have to learn to crawl.
Mutate your gills, develop lungs
know your place, you have no land,
you are an alien species.
Forget the borders, tie up your tongue
here you are safe – between the walls of this place.
Stay put for now, We will decide –
wait
     w a i t
          w a i t
               w a i t
W
   A
     I
          T

Resilience

The freedom to be who you are.
Without, within.

When I learnt to respect
this island – my body –
its creative boundaries
and endless possibilities,
when I became aware
of the shimmering breath
on its surface,
I smiled.

Like Gulliver in Lilliput
laughing about the minority complex
of the crowds or the narcissistic pride
of the powerful, embedded in
the realism of materialism,
I still crossed borders but now invisibly
not as a victim of legal agreements
between nations, but as the heroine
of my novel, my own creation –
the plot I was the mistress of.

It took thirty years and then
as the ironic twist of this particular
story – a pandemic struck.

Will we ever be free?
Or my boundaries cannot be
surmounted for I have skin
and spit –

and yet we had to find
ways – and learnt the art
of smiling
with the eyes.

The Journalist – for Nedim Türfent

Artery that carries blood from the nation's heart
through the whole body to the smallest member
so the nation's heart can welcome back
the life lived and renew it, all the nation's blood.
This is the ideal. We fail but we get up again,
carrying life, in words, to our brothers, sisters... nations.

Nedim Türfent is a Kurdish journalist who was arrested by Turkish authorities in 2016 for reporting on Turkish special police forces' ill-treatment of Turkish and Kurdish workers. He is still in prison. PEN International, Wales PEN Cymru and Irish PEN are among those organisations campaigning for his release.

The Sanctuary

Not metal railings. Briars of thick mottled marble barred the way
and steps, one on the other, insisted on an effortful ascent.
God lived on that altar – never slept, said the two red, wakeful lamps.
He was there inside a domed brass tabernacle whose doors, if opened,
opened onto curtains so you never could see in,
and behind, above, purples and magentas, perplexed and broken,
toppled around His pinioned son. The Son was always dying.
God's hand, at the apex, open-palmed, proffered
the only – irrelevant – stabs of light.
The likes of us stood well away, not to get burned.
Women especially. He let them clean the steps
and the marble-panelled walls, heads down.
This was power, and unapproachability. This was God.

Sometimes a phrase just turns you over.
It's a corner that you walk around and everything
opens up. The previous falls away:
always about Him – His sanctuary, His place.
Instead, it's 'where God's people come
to know that they are loved'.

Attending

You wanted an impresario, compelling the people's awed obedience,
a power demonstrable and apt. God evaded you. He turned
from the paths you had marked out for Him. He stepped away
from arguments and proof. He moved
to a silence that you couldn't bear.

But one who is silent long enough compels attention.
You leant in, fell, and sank through fathom after fathom,
seeing how differently the light refracted there.
Storms could be felt as rocking shifts of weight, and time
passed over the surface like a wind.

You had to acknowledge you were sunk
and God spoke then. He said, *Sit here with me.*
All I want is this attentiveness. It lets me in.
You are my home; my sanctuary, where I can be
who I am. Tell them this waiting is the opening of the door.

Annunciation, Visitation

After the angel left her what was the girl to do?
I see her stand, go to the window,
look out at the utterly familiar street.
A neighbour, jovial, passes and she smiles
— too soon for speech. She looks down
at her utterly familiar hand
resting on the white stone sill.

Even the Ark of the Covenant, Tower of Ivory,
House of Gold needs time. Her fingers, tendons, wrist
all look the same and yet, freighted
with all futures and their origin, with someone
beyond time, she has become a sanctuary.

What she is to do has been left
to her. That mention of a cousin's pregnancy
in the distant uplands, seems suddenly a path.
She turns, sweeping her former future
from the sill, brushing her hands together.
Joseph she'll tell when she gets back,
three months well in.

She was so full of grace the reverberation
of a word could topple her into flow.
Words never work with us. We are too dry.
But the knock behind the breast-bone
as an embryonic someone
leaps to greet the wordless Virgin
of the Glimpse… that suddenly open door…
shakes us to tears.
We call it wind-scour, cloud-scape,
know it to be more.

After Iconoclasm
1: A Reflection on Technique

The emptied niche is a womb,
perpetually conceiving,
and the great window, burst,
a stone-stringed larynx
and the gouge-marks on the eyes of saints
record in ogham
how their gaze held the wielder of the knife
and called him, 'Cain',
for it's always murder, of the life
the image veils
(hence the requirement for official
sanctioning)
so the icon-breaker is advised
to leave no trace:
no frescoed drapery, no elegant
plaster shoe,
no painted personhood, and especially
no space
– headless torso, alcove
or pedestal –
nothing that calls for something.

After Iconoclasm
2: Annunciation Re-assembled

Llanfair, Yr Wyddgrug / Church of the Virgin Mary, Mold

I could fear an angel who descends,
majestic, like the Prince he is,
bearing a tremendous invitation
through the loggia that frames him
in a garden all enclosed
but this angel of Yr Wyddgrug
is Prince only of shards.

His Virgin we must infer
from this piece of blue
and the Spirit from — is that a bird? —
askew as a broken compass.

This Gabriel of Wales speeds,
a comet heading eastward,
his hair streaming behind him
in a cosmic wind.
'*Such an eager face.*'
All that remains of him.

Enough for us to glimpse
the threshold of that girl's reply.

After Iconoclasm
3: The Jesse Tree Window

Llanrhaeadr yng Nghinmeirch / Church by the waterfall in the region of the ridge of horses

The window spilled across the floor
and yet was whole.
We walked on amethyst and ochre
— technology abashed —
lifting our eyes to a half-millennium of light
as the cameraman was drenched in rose
and the sound recordist's mouth, a silent O,
said the awe of generations.
Then the blink, to focus to perfection
the imperfections in this wall of glass
until we grasped that, when the Terror loomed,
love disappeared the Jesse Tree
and brought it back — in time —
in places crazed
as the zealot's bliss,
as the ice-sheet over the abyss.
Undaunted, aureoled in boughs,
the young Queen lifts her Child —
    Breakable Saviour
    Dauntingly Powerless Power.

After Iconoclasm
4: Defaced Angel Holding Defaced Souls

Southwold

God side-lined me while his reiving angels rode,
while the sickle was put in, and the threshing flail
and the winnowing fan cut right and left
and the strippers of trees and seas roared
through creation. *Now*, he said, *fold up your wings*
so you can stoop under the apple boughs.
He handed me a cloth the width of an embrace
and sent me out. It was the evening of that day.
Above me emptied branches rocked.
The moon had fallen but the stars clung on.
I walked by my own radiance and gathered, from underfoot,
windfalls — tumbled, damaged, scattered in grass,
huddled among stones. When the cloth was full
as a gleaning housewife's apron, God
removed my face and named me,
Angel of the Faceless, of the unrecorded,
those who dropped and rolled away un-heeded,
who receive, at this last hour.... Here
I forestalled him. I opened the cloth
and poured my harvest into his lap.

After Iconoclasm
5: A Teenage Tartan Gang Member in St. Anthony's Roman Catholic Church, Belfast, February 6th 1973

I always picture him as half-way down the aisle,
frozen suddenly, as the others thunder past
towards the shallow steps that hem a place
he has no name for.
The altar he does know, now that he sees one,
and how they swarm it – bending its gleaming cross
from head to toe while someone jemmies open
its golden cupboard.
He'd relished the bounding up the steps outside,
the mighty push to breach the massive doors,
the surge into the porch – unstoppable, even
by its man-on-a-cross.
Hands were laid on, that plaster idol wrenched
down, trampled, and they were through the inner doors
into a raftered, eerie, night-filled space
he had no name for,
nor for the wall of shadowy figures up ahead,
nor for the black explosions in the ribs and chest
and shins of its brittle Christ who was dying again,
nor for the energy
unleashed on the long-haired girl in tears at those feet.
Someone is flinging white confetti from a goblet:
'*This is their god!*' Someone orders him to shoulder
a wooden bench
out to the flames. He stumbles on the wreckage in the porch
and falls. In dreams, he feels again that fall
and gives a name to breaking it with the heel
of his hand on a face.

After Iconoclasm
6: The Chapel of the Trees

Worshipping here, I read from the rubric of my helplessness,
beginning, as must every Mass, with a confession of my guilt:
collusion, failure to admonish, heeding a counsel of despair.
The enemy is legion and has lodged himself within me
so that I do – not what I want. I do what wounds me and the world.

The trees are nothing but themselves while I let myself be warped
away from true. How mighty are their crowns – an intermediate heaven.
At their feet how small I am, and petty the thrones I clamber to
on ladders of cheap self-interest to make myself look big.

One day my flesh will feed the trees – atonement of a kind –
but even now my gaze on these icons of the good, the steadfast
and the pure opens a path on which their essence moves
towards me, helping me pledge reform and restoration,
helping them teach their fellow-creature how to flourish.

A Gardener Imagines Death During the Pandemic, 2020

Is this what I will see:
against a haze of blue a yellow iris
— spear among green blades —
calling me upwards from my final stumble?
No time to name them, each one
and everything I've loved, but a yellow
that is all that *yellow* is
assuming me. Or
eyes behind a visor, summoning me
to all that *human* is?

In Early Lockdown: Antrim

I've made a Spring bouquet for you, my love,
of gorse. *Harsh!* you'll recoil. *For this harsh time?*
Yes, and not yes. It's true gorse is a glove
of blood for any hand, a paradigm
of touch-me-not, a keep-your-distance hedge.
Gorse 'bears it out even to the edge of doom',
endures, defends, fends off the slightest touch.
Why? For the sake of its exotic bloom:
a golden purse, sheathed in pistachio green,
that flings its riches to the cloudy skies
till Ireland swoons, drenched in a heady rain
of tropical perfume, a paradise.
I will be gorse while we are kept apart,
with you The Land of Spices in my

die

you might

die in an ICU

and I would never
get to kiss you ever
again my breath might
be your ruin I am afraid afraid afraid
but that very
iamb in my chest it says
be brave be brave and be
the lover that the times require,
giving and taking

heart.

Vision, North Antrim, in the Aftermath of Lockdown

The Carrickmore Road hems my parish of Culfeightrin
where its townlands – Broughanlea, Drumaroan, Tornabodagh,
   Tornaroan –
dip their skirts into the Sea of Moyle,
        with a last flounce of grassy clefts, precarious caravans
        and a beading of white houses
before relinquishing themselves
to waves that take the colour of the sky, a jumbled grey.

Here all is profusely, wetly, Irishly grey or green;
even the light arrives through a dampened veil yet
pagoda roofs, crimson
– the hedges are full of them.
Each dangles a furl of imperial purple,
a firework spurting tiny comets
down to a mossy sky.

That veil's dissolving. I see
sulphur-yellow sunbursts in the ditch;
hard globes of military red strung on the bushes
for a brash tattoo; cockades – vermilion –
tossed up among the brambles by a hidden crowd;
medals of cerise pinned to the ferny cliffs; corsages of
hot mauve, burnt orange, the colour *lucifer*...

Is it because I've reached this edge
that I have eyes at last to see
what has been burning always
within my coolest day?
After these months of paring-down, let me keep
my vision stripped,
here, where there is no further north.

In This Sanctuary
Viviana Fiorentino

You blue tit, jackdaw or young doe
you, overflow, the breaker of borders
of species, you know it will not matter
that you were males or females, your voice

is

singing

        you feel devastation

is

growing

/it's only after our hands have travelled up
and down all over our own body now

in this sanctuary adhering
to an invisible current
between the two contemplating
and the act of separating/

listen to
this never-ending twine a particle
a whole body made of white roots,
hands of water, sea arms pushing
to the nucleus of rocks

and the legs
stretch
out – to the sky – cloud

and blue.

There Must Be Somewhere

that is safe from violation.
Childhood. Being son, or daughter. Pregnancy,
old age, infirmity – none of these.

The corridors of hospitals, asylums, refuges
– places we thought were sacrosanct –
are roamed by predators

and though the innocent fox has his earth
and the birds of the air their nests, we are un-homing
ourselves and ravaging even our own minds.

Yet we hope for sanctuary, a nook out of the wind,
shelter in the *cwtch* of someone's overcoat,
a harbouring gaze, if nothing else.

I often think about that song, *The Parting Glass*.
The last toast raised, the one who has to leave
steps out, across the threshold, into the turbulent night;

that brilliant room
(where the worst of him was known, forgiven, shouldered)
remains his compass, carried always.

Nowhere is safe. We know that.
And we know that somewhere is
because we've been there, irrefutably,

and we can find it,
open its door,
return to the welcome that we left.

Welsh *cwtch* – a close and warm embrace / a small safe space

Home

As I spoke, I realised that he was listening,
that he had opened up some room inside himself
and there was the hallway beckoning me
towards a door, giving onto a sunlit living space
that I could enter, my burden in my arms,
and when I'd placed it on his table
we would, together, loosen its bonds,
consider it... quietly.

What we were talking of I don't remember now
but that he, on his threshold, stood aside to let me in
— that has never left me. He gave me living proof
that this is how we're meant to be,
capable of choosing to welcome someone in,
and that when that person does the same for us
he is our shelter. We are a home for one another.
And this holds true for everyone.

The Poets

MAHYAR

Mahyar is an Iranian now living in Wales.

GLEN WILSON

Glen Wilson is a multi-award winning and widely published poet from Portadown. He won the Seamus Heaney Award for New Writing in 2017, the Jonathan Swift Creative Writing Award in 2018 and The Trim Poetry competition in 2019.

He was commissioned by the Irish Football Association to write poems for the Northern Ireland Football team. These have appeared on Sky Sports. He has recently been shortlisted for the Ó Bhéal Five Words Competition, The Ken Saro-Wiwa Poetry competition and the Dalkey Creates Writing competition and won the Padraic Fallon Poetry competition and Slipstream Open Poetry competition in 2021. His poetry collection *An Experience on the Tongue* is out now with Doire Press. He is currently working towards his second collection.

PHIL COPE

Cardiff-born Phil Cope is a writer, photographer, and exhibition and book designer. His 2021 book, *The Golden Valley, a visual biography of the Garw* (where he lives) was published by Seren, which also published his *Holy Wells Cornwall* (2010); *Holy Wells Scotland* (2015) and *The Living Wells of Wales* (2019). His next book will be on the holy wells of Ireland.

As a teacher of Drama and English Phil spent two years as the principal of an isolated Algonkin Native Indian Reserve college in Northern Canada; taught at the Shah of Iran's Imperial Court in Tehran and in Wales, Greece and Haiti. In 1980 he set up Valley and Vale, Wales' largest community arts team, which he led for sixteen years.

Increasingly, Phil likes to work collaboratively. *Sanctuary* follows three other joint ventures: *The Dancing Pilgrimage of Water* with the late Dewi Roberts (2010); *Sacred North* with Fr John Musther (2018) and *The Man Who Gave His Horse To A Beggar* (Aidan of Lindisfarne) with John Connell (2020).

CSILLA TOLDY

Csilla was born in Budapest. Her film scripts won international awards such as the Hartley-Merril, Big Break and Katapult Prizes. As a video artist, she creates award-winning video poems. Her publications include UK and Irish literary magazines and anthologies, such as *Southword, The Black Mountain Review, The Incubator* and *Ink Sweat and Tears, The Stony Thursday Book, The Honest Ulsterman, Crannóg, Cyphers, Pamenar Magazine* and the *Journal of Transnational Writing.* Her poetry readings are included in the Irish Poetry Archive of UCD Library. She published three poetry books with Lapwing Publications Belfast (2013, 2015, 2018). Her poetry was anthologised by Demeter Press (CAN), Dedalus, Arlen House (ROI), and Recent Works Press (AU). Her short story collection, *Angel Fur* was published by Stupor Mundi in 2019. Her debut novel, *Bed, Table, Door* is forthcoming with Wrecking Ball Press in 2022. Csilla lives in Northern Ireland.

VIVIANA FIORENTINO

Viviana Fiorentino is a bilingual poet based in Belfast, originally from Italy. She is Lecturer in Italian at IIC Dublin and facilitator at Quotidian Word on the Street. She published a novel and two poetry collections in Italy (*In giardino* (Controluna Edizioni); *Trasferimenti* (Zona Contemporanea); *Tra mostri ci si ama* (Transeuropa Edizioni). Her poems in English have appeared in various international literature magazines and in anthologies. Some of her poems have been recorded for the Irish Poetry Reading Archive. She co-founded three Irish poetry projects: Sky, You Are Too Big, A Suitcase of Poetry and Letters With Wings. Viviana is on the editorial board of Le Ortique, a blog and initiative that wants to rediscover forgotten women artists. She is a board member of Irish PEN.

ANGELA GRAHAM

Angela Graham is from Belfast. She had a long and distinguished career in TV and cinema in Wales. She was Development Producer on the BBC series *The Story of Wales* presented by Huw Edwards (2 BAFTA Cymru Awards). She was producer and co-writer of the Oscar entrant cinema feature *Branwen* (6 BAFTA Cymru nominations and Best Film at the Celtic Media Festival). Her short story collection *A City Burning* (Seren 2020) was longlisted for the Edge Hill Prize. Her poems have been published widely in journals such as *The North, Poetry Wales, The Interpreter's House* and often anthologised, most recently in *Local Wonders* (Dedalus Press) *Words From The Brink* and *A470* (Arachne Press) and *Washing Windows Too* (Arlen House).

Acknowledgements

I'd like to thank the five 'Sanctuary' poets for their engagement and generosity. Working with them opened up a range of experience far beyond my own. My particular thanks are due to Glen Wilson for his mentoring and to Phil Cope for his photographs on the back cover. I'm grateful to Amy Wack, former poetry editor at Seren for her belief in me as a poet, and to Damian Smyth, Head of Literature and Drama at the Arts Council of Northern Ireland for his insight and guidance. My thanks to Matthew M.C. Smith and Swansea Asylum Seekers Support who introduced me to Mahyar; to Dr Philip Robinson for his ever-generous help on the nuances of Ulster-Scots and to the many other proponents of it; to Dr Sharon Jones and Rhian Sykes and her colleagues in physiotherapy at University Hospital Wales for helping to keep me going; to Elena Ciuplea for making many practical things possible Many organisations which support refugees and asylum seekers in Wales and Northern Ireland generously shared their experiences. My thanks go also to Publisher Mick Felton and the team at Seren. Most of all my thanks go to my husband, John Geraint for unfailing support and encouragement.

Several poems have appeared in magazines and anthologies: *The Honest Ulsterman, Wales Arts Review, The Lonely Crowd, Shamrocks and Shells, The Stony Thursday Book, Silver Branch* (Black Bough Poetry), *Heartland Penfro Anthology* (Parthian Books), *Winners of the Ulster-Scots Writing Competition 2021* (Linen Hall Library), *Local Wonders* (Dedalus Press).

'A Gardener Imagines Death During The Pandemic' appeared in the online project pendemic.ie 2020, as did an earlier version of 'In Early Lockdown: Antrim' which also appeared in pestilencepoems.blogspot.com 2020